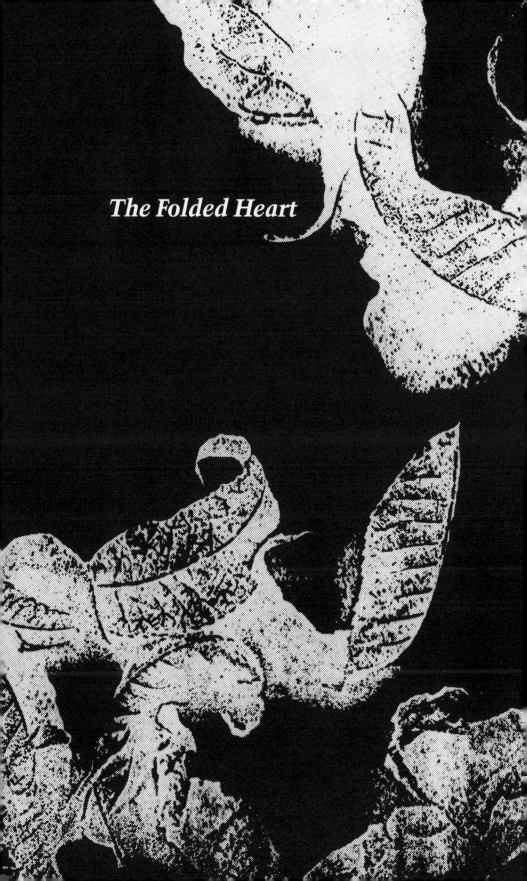

The Folded Heart

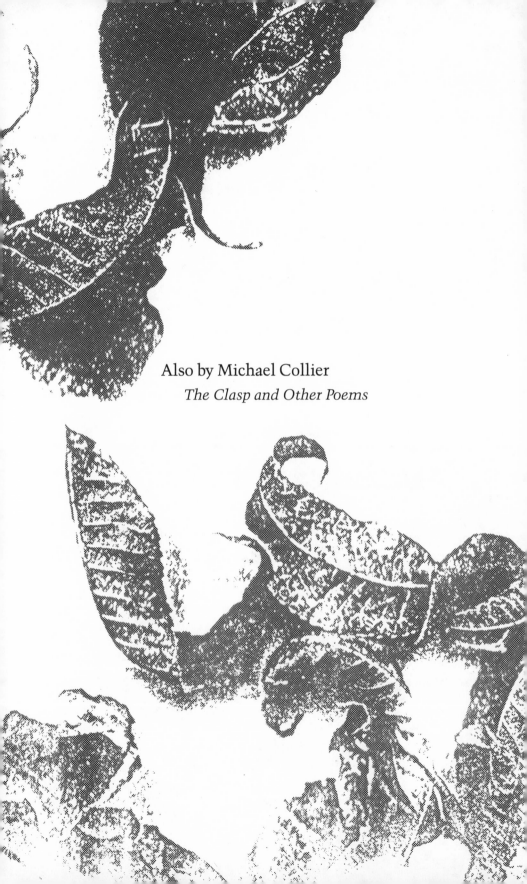

Also by Michael Collier

The Clasp and Other Poems

The Folded Heart

Michael Collier

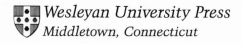 Wesleyan University Press
Middletown, Connecticut

Some of the poems in this book originally appeared in *Agni Review,*
American Poetry Review, Antaeus, Boulevard, The Missouri Review,
Partisan Review, Ploughshares, Raccoon, The Reaper, and *TriQuarterly.*
"Feedback" originally appeared in *The New Yorker;* "The Diver," "A
Private Place," and "Tonight" in *Poetry.*

I would like to thank Edward Hirsch, Garrett Hongo, William Meredith,
John Murphy, Elizabeth Spires, and David St. John for their friendship
and encouragement.

Grants from the National Endowment for the Arts and the Graduate
School of the University of Maryland made possible many of the
poems in the book.

All inquiries and permissions requests should be addressed to the
Publisher, Wesleyan University Press, 110 Mt. Vernon Street, Middletown,
Connecticut 06457

Library of Congress Cataloging-in-Publication Data

Collier, Michael.
  The folded heart.

  (Wesleyan poetry)
  I. Title. II. Series
PS3553.0474645F6 1989   811'.54   88–28090
ISBN 0–8195–2169–8
ISBN 0–8195–1171–4 (pbk.)

Manufactured in the United States of America

First Edition

Wesleyan Poetry

For Katherine

Contents

The Folded Heart

The Problem

Awake in the dark, I counted the planes
that hung by thumbtacks and string from the ceiling.

I brought them out of their shadows with their names:
Hellcat, Spitfire, Messerschmitt and Zero.

They were part of a problem that made death fair.

Part promise, part gamble, the problem went like this:
How old must I be before I am old enough for my father to die?

The answer was always twenty-one—
a number impossible to imagine.

It made the world fair enough for sleep.

My father didn't die when I was twenty-one.
I didn't blame him. He didn't know that night after night

I had bargained his life away for sleep.

Now to calm my fear of my father's death,
I remember the delicate plastic landing gear

of those airplanes, their sharp axles protruding
from the hard gray tires. You had to be careful

with the noxious glue. You had to put one drop
of it on a difficult place and then blow lightly

until the tire began to spin.

1

Skimming

It was nothing more than a summer job,
hopping the low fence to my neighbor's house,
where I paid out the long hollow pole
through my hands, and dipped the skimmer's
blue jaw into the pool to strain
the insect wings, bird feathers
and carob leaves that lay like the night's

siftings on a huge blue mirror.
Evenings from our patio next door,
I heard my neighbors thrashing
in the shallow end, their voices
wild in the cool element, their feet
padding heavily over the concrete deck.
And later, in darkness, they slipped back

into the green water silently.
The yellow glow of the citronella candle
flickering far away through the oleanders.
Its oily lemon fragrance heavy in the air.
Sometimes I heard the woman crying, sometimes
the man, and once I heard a gasp
as dry and sharp and loud as someone

taking a last breath before he drowns.
Some mornings I'd find the pool light
burning faintly in the deep end,
the surface covered with all that was attracted
to the submerged glow, and once I found
a bat floating in the shallow pocket
of the stairs. Its wings spread out

like a Gothic W. Its feet angling
from its belly like a ship's screws.
And lifting the black mass gently from the water,
turning the skimmer over in the grass,
I tapped the bat out and let it lie face up
in the morning sun. Its features
like a rubber mask's, reddish, roughened,

as if its passage out of the attic or cave
had been difficult and the twilight air
of the neighborhood provided nothing more
than blue shadow on blue shadow.

V-8

The motor hung in my neighbor's back yard
for years, tarp-covered and lashed with rope.
Suspended from the rusty block and tackle
of an engine hoist, it cast a constant shadow
on the concrete pad. And all around it lay
the necklaces and hoses of its accessories:
the black spark-plug harness, the bedpan
of the air filter, the fuel pump and distributor,
the carburetor on its side with its barrels
and chambers exposed. And though my neighbor

never rebuilt the engine, he must have thought
about it often: a heavy pendulum that
no wind moved, a plumb bob fixed dead center
like some bulky reference point he ducked
and dodged each time he passed through the yard.
And each time, too, he had to pass the small side
door to the garage which held the silent tools:
the bright chrome sockets and ratchets, wrenches
and drivers bundled in soft canvas, like good silver
shoed in its polish cloth. I was too young to know

what a life's work was, too impatient to understand
how our true affections are deflected, shunted
by the domestic, by the hard promises we make
to another. What did I know of our capacity to transform
bitterness into love, as he did helping
a teenager load the V-8 into the back of a pickup,
cranking the hoist winch down slowly with one hand
and with the other fending off the willful spin of the block,
until it settled in the bed, tilted on its side,
leaking a puddle of oil, dark and latent?

Iodine

The cure-all bottle fits the palm
of his hand, and the rubber nipple
of the squeeze top rises like a black
thumb in the shadow of his thumb.

Skull and crossbones on the label,
and the wide morgue of the medicine
cabinet open. The order of gauze,
tape and cotton on the glass shelves.

The flesh-colored bandage held
in a tight roll by its butterfly clasp.
Dusting of talc. Flocking of toothpaste.
The white soft ridges of soap in the empty

dish. And his other hand under the rush of cold
water. The sink filling with rosy, thinned
blood. The blue razor blade he was trying
to fit into the cabinet's disposal slot

lies like a fish fin on the pink ceramic counter.
Then resting the cut hand on the rim of the sink,
fingers held up to slow the flow of blood,
my uncle fits the bottle in his mouth.

The exaggerated squint of one eye
as his teeth tighten on the plastic cap
and his good hand strains, like a wrench,
until the seal on the vial breaks. Then his tongue,

ferrous with the leakage, sputters and spits,
his lips wiping the bitterness on his shoulder,
the back of his wrist. His head crazy
with the mistake. And the water he cups

in his hands, brackish with blood and iodine,
is the color of the veil that shrouds
his life and its absurd diminishment
there in the bathroom of his sister's house.

The Pageant

When Brian McCarthy, the male lead
in our third-grade, Spanish-class
production of *Alice in Wonderland*,

didn't show, Mrs. Carrera's husband,
Tito, had to read lines from the wings,
where he also managed the plywood

and canvas scenery. Paunchy in a white
T-shirt, sleeves covering tattooed anchors,
he lost whole sentences in drapery

and screens, which made Alice, the precocious
Diane Grasso, bossier than ever, more confident,
so that she served up tildes and rolled

r's like virtuoso yo-yo tricks.
The pageant made city news in the morning paper:
a photograph framed by the ratty proscenium

of the social hall, in which Mrs. Carrera
occupies the foreground, holding
her blue-and-red velveteen

needlepoint portrait of Kennedy
(her scapular of gratitude for America)
while the cast stands by height

in tiers behind her, and Tito out of sight
in the wings smokes in his folding chair,
a hand on the drapery cords, his feet

propped on the tiny canvas door he made
for Alice.

A Private Place

I kept you buried in a shallow alley grave,
a hollowed dirt canoe, in which after having touched
your legs and breasts and shoulders,
I rolled you up like a sporting program—
a telescope or megaphone—through which I could
see or speak to you when you were gone.

I dug you up as often as I thought of you,
though sometimes I'd resist and so my giving in
was sweeter. And even now I remember
you were the band leader's lead singer,
puffery of sex, your mermaid torso shimmering
and s-ing from the wings along the chorus's

harmonious edge and holding the big bulb-headed
microphone, cleavage high, like black broccoli.
I found you in a neighbor's garbage, buried
like something that could never hide, and later
when you were fast leaving me for the damp earth,
targets of mold and mildew eating through you,

I knew I'd have to give you up. Obsessions hurt
like death, and part of who we are dies when part
of what we want dulls and disintegrates, and the earth's
powdery talc obscures our keen desires with time.
And so I thought to lie down next to you as in some
foxhole and smell the moist iron of the ground.

Lagoon

Four or five of us stripped to our underwear,
bobbing in the dark. The acrid stench
of mud and sulfur. And then clouds closing
over the moon above. Rain pocking
the surface, and a silence, separate from

the grassy banks, sand traps and palm trees
that hissed and darkened with the stinging rain.
Steam rose everywhere. Our feet in the clayey
ooze. Patches of algae floating to the top.
And our treading in the murk for a few golf balls,

with their shiny black or red script,
their covers smooth and perfect or gashed
and contused with their dark creases and miles
of rubber band wound round the small ball
in the center—black as a fish eye,

inky as a hideous gland. And at the center
of the lagoon that thing we were drifting down
toward, our legs as white as roots,
reaching slowly and blindly for anchor,
we never found, for always back of the rain, back

of our wish to drown, we could hear the whirr
of the watchman's Cushman, see his search-
light sweep fairways and hazards,
hear the bone crunch of tires over gravel paths
and the pounding of his dog set loose.

The stiff-legged shepherd that broke through
the oleanders lining the irrigation ditch
to find us scaling the supple web of the chain link
fence, the high visible screen that surrounded the golf
course and trapped the dog in the domain of his fury.

The Brothers

For thirty-five cents, they sold me
a homing pigeon and promised
to care for it in the ramshackle
quarters of their pigeon coop,
and that whenever I wanted to see it,
I could telephone and they would release
the bird for its flight to me,
its true home.

I was nine and small and white,
uncertain as I stood on the back porch
while Tito, Mike and Carlos pointed
to the brown-and-white one with red
stitched in its neck, and though
I could not find it, as everyone else could,
I nodded, afraid they'd make me
hold my ugly bird.

And how many times after I telephoned
did I sit in my back yard and looking
into the sky, hardly knowing sparrow
from pigeon, did I wait, believing
that each bird passing by
was mine, or if not mine,
then released into the air
for its passage home?

I wish now they had made me
hold my bird and learn
that I could keep it calm
and reconcile the frantic pressure
of its wings against my palms,
for twenty years have passed and I feel
the absence of something
I never held.

Though it wasn't absence, finally,
that made me demand my pigeon,
calling the brothers thieves and liars
from where I stood in the alley.
But the brothers never answered me,
and I could see through the weave
of fence palings that the coop
was empty, though the evening light

had made its passage
through the wiry geometry of the cage,
had calmed itself,
and then dissolved.

Feedback

You are down on your knees, but you are not praying.
You are holding the hollow body
of your cherrywood Gretsch Tennessean
guitar across your thighs,

and you are pressing the right side of your face
against the black grille of the Fender Bandmaster amp
whose ruby pilot light glows like a planet in the dark.
You are listening to the last chord that fades into the black

cone of the speaker, which is ridged and grooved
like the walls of Hell and leaves only a ghost vibration
in your ear. And you are waiting for your friend to lower
the tone arm of the black plastic GE Stereo

onto the grooves of the record so you can imitate
Blue Cheer, Quicksilver, Jefferson Airplane,
and curve your shoulders over the guitar like a bird
holding its wings in glide, while your friend

rocks and jerks, gives himself over to the pulse
that drives you deeper and deeper
to the center of your teenage hearts. You are raw
and born for the distortion that lives beyond your ears

in the darkness, and is too loud with fuzztone
and wah-wah pedal. And each note or chord you strike
in imitation is partially saved, suspended,
as you pull and pump the vibrato's thin blade

and stir the molecules of sound as your long hair
obscures your faces, and you recede deeper, more separate,
into your selves here in this world, on this earth,
in the converted garage with its brown Georgia-Pacific

paneling and green burlap curtains that hang
above the avocado-green carpet.

2

North Corridor

Living along the path
of these inconstant tracks
(a spur for shuttling coal),

we've learned to anticipate
the freight that pounds
at night and shakes our home

and stays in us as a dream
of something heavy stays,
foreboding and proximate

but always passing through.
So when a single boxcar
strayed one morning, chalk-

scrawled with siding codes,
creaking and sighing,
but also jingling like coins

in a collection box, we left
our house to stare at it.
And where it came to rest,

a prisoner of the crossing gates,
it stayed until the afternoon—
unclaimed, inscrutable,

locked with metal sealing tape.
Cars shunted around it,
over the rails. Children scaled

its laddered sides and hung
from its chain-locked wheel brake
and fit their necks inside

the couplings' claw-shaped
handcuffs. They did it
for a thrill, for fun,

though no one laughed. Then
in the afternoon two railway men
appeared in their blue truck

and carried long pole pry-jacks
to the wheels and slipped
the iron tongues along the rails

until with only their bodies
they fulcrummed the boxcar
to move just off the crossing,

where it stayed until that night.
When we heard the thrashing, the screech
of metal stretching from the dark

tree-thick right-of-way, it was as if
the mother of us all had come
to claim us, angry, staring us down

with her bright headlight, then butting
our heads, staggering the whole house
behind the engine's sudden lurch.

Burial

As if to prove death benefits the world
of protocols and attendants, the small
white headstones curve in beautiful arcs
over these green and gentle, tree-spaced
hills. Oak and beech and poplar drop
their leaves like service bars, bronze
and red and gold as thick as the gilded
leaf-scroll on the adjutant's visor.

The thick oak casket lies under a white
makeshift shed. The family sits in rows
of metal folding chairs. They are close
enough to touch the black valance that drops
in pleats beneath the coffin, but their hands
would have to pass between the legs of eight
men in long black coats. The men stand
tense and wound, like cocked winches, and hold

the flag that's stretched as tight as steel
yet floats above the casket like an illusionist's
wife. Up the hill musicians play taps.
The tuba turns to catch the sun and shines
like a brass air vent. Farther up
the hill white gloves slide up rifle stocks,
slam bolts shut and aim the barrels high.
Before the rifles' sharp reports,

the barrels bloom with smoke
and in the short delay, the dead man
is meant to pass from this world
to the next, though surely he's been gone
for days and returns now for the pure
circumstance, the final ceremony
that has the flag become his heart,
folded in its bulky triangle and handed

to his wife, who knows she's not to look
but, rather, lays it on her lap
and puts her hands on top and presses down
as if to keep the loud heart from beating loud.

Air Guitar

Is it me there
in the young clerk
at the Circle-K
holding the neck
of an invisible guitar,

whose rock music
rises above explosions
of a Star Wars game?
Or am I standing, years
before, stoned in front

of a band, working frets,
revving strings?
Something flashes in the
cash register's bluish
green digits, but what's

the difference? The song
the clerk moves against
I left minutes before
in a bar, or years ago
sang to myself—vase for a

microphone—in my own room.
Who was it I wanted
to become miming rock stars,
or tonight in a bar
or when holding a woman

and not feeling her? I remember
someone turning to me
in the black light
and strobe flash of a high-
school dance to say, "Heh,

we're air guitarists, man."
His teeth bright as piano
keys hung in the air
as he smiled, while the white
so shimmered it shook free

of itself, broke over us
as our bodies
disappeared in the strobe's
intervals. The music
we squeezed from our fingers

hung in the air, then fell
or exploded as space ships
explode now in the Circle-K.
A kid tracking the universe
for notes sent out

a decade ago. Locking in
on the past, vaporizing
the pulses of light it embodies.
And in the bar was it me
telling the woman I played

guitar to explain my
fingers pressed in the heel
of my palm? Who is it
pushing away the clerk's
reflection that hangs full-length

in the glass doors as I leave?
Who is it in the mute light
of the parking lot wanting
to remember a better self,
proficient in the past?

Practicing Stalls

Long ago you lay in your back yard
listening to planes circle
for the dirt strip near your house.
They droned loudly at first, but when
they throttled back, almost to silence,
your heart stopped for a moment.

Though you couldn't see the planes
and after a while there was only the
sound of your breath near sleep,
in that instant when your heart stopped,
something uncontrolled and heavy
began falling in you: a sense that a life

had passed nearby, or the falling
you already knew from dreams, or the completely
imaginable kind that kept you from jumping
off the roof. Whichever, a space opened,
and you quieted so as not to miss
the crash that never came.

* * *

Now when the propeller's blade unwinds
like a broken film and floods the cockpit
with the sudden bright light of a projection lamp,
your heart stops. Wind blows through the engine
cowling, beats the Plexiglas like a desperate
hand and a voice says, *Let me in before I fall,*

and falling, you hear another voice rise
to its last plea, *Let me in*. You trim
the elevators, and the nose rises to a saving
attitude. You practice stalls again and again
until everyone is safe.

* * *

Years from now you may lie in your back yard
and through half-closed eyes watch
the flat jets too high to be heard
leave their white trails behind, and though
friends of yours have died, and you haven't
yet stopped dreaming of falling, you know
that when a propeller unwinds and a voice
cries, *Let me in*, it is your own death
that spins as slowly as a blade before you.
It's not like the beginning near the dirt strip,
or when practicing stalls: you could lose
all that altitude and never fall.

Tonight

As you look from your office
into the intersection below,
the dull smudge of a barber's shop
is wedged between the glittery front
of a punk boutique and a chain bookstore
with its collage of dust-jacket displays.

And looking down after a day
in front of a computer screen,
your eyes having tracked the white cursor
as it made its soft imprints and erasures,
it is difficult to imagine the people
below as anything more than pulses of light
moving toward destinations that are mostly emotional:

magnitudes of happiness derived from a haircut
or the skewed brashness of wearing
a T-shirt that displays an obscenity
in Japanese or the heavy certainty
of a book about Poland or Space,
subjects as vast and indisputable
as the street emptying now because
it's begun to rain or because
of people like you, held back from
destinations, who can no longer
see themselves in the teenage couple

standing in the recess of the corner bank
where they sway in clumsy love
as the white light of the automatic teller
hangs at their chests
while the girl plays distractedly
with the luminous keys.

The Grandmothers

1.
She strayed in the hall
untethered from her room
loose in the air, available
to any name I might call.
Wingless in her picked-at
sweater, Grandmother sat with me
and nodded and held her hands
with her hands, listening
to something I couldn't hear.

And so intent, she stood as if
commanded and clapped her hands
and then sat down, and then stood up
until her minions in their
white hats came, not angry,
but to lead their angel
out of the confusing light
that broke in her hands.

2.
We have just left Aura singing
awash on a raft of white sheets.
When we came she was propped
in her wheelchair cawing
like a white bird with broken wings,
blinking and chirping, nervous,
unsure of her keepers.

When she saw us walk through the door,
she quieted like a child
who has finally woken her parents
and now must say there is nothing

wrong, only a dream that scared her,
only a fear of forever being alone.
But she was blind without her glasses

that lay unfolded in her lap,
and so she quieted to hear us
whispering her name as if through
the weave of a bamboo cage
to a bird so exotic and delicate
we were afraid she might fly away.

Winter, 1959

I still watch the ice accrue crystal by crystal
around their orange vests and hats,
rifle barrels turning blue and black then white
and their bodies like a snow fence
stop the drifts and form a mound
whose holdings no one would suspect.

My hope was that sheathed in ice
they'd stay intact until the spring,
untouched by animals, when someone's breath
or sifting dust would bring them back to life
and that their beard-dark faces would appear
rescued out of ice, in the newspaper.

I wanted the world to save its greatest patience
for their corpses, that lying grouped
or scattered on some wrong trail, they would not
disassemble easily, but would rise up and see
the trees shelving away to the campground
and their small green tents that had collapsed under snow.

And though no one ever found them, no one's ever called
them *dead*. Always they've been *lost*, as if the ice
would melt, the snow blow back into the sky
and their footprints lead the rescue party
to a bonfire or a snow cave like a room of glass
that filled and held their shallow, patient breath.

The Heavy Light of Shifting Stars

Some times the nite is the shape of a ear only it ain't
a ear we know the shape of.
　　　　　　—Russell Hoban, *Riddley Walker*

The huge magnanimous stars are many things.
At night we lower window shades
to mute the sparkling circuitry of the universe;
at day the sun's clear mist, like beautiful
cabinetry, shrouds the workings of the sky.

Everything is hidden, everything is apparent,
so that light coming toward us, held
in the faces of our old regrets, is blue;
while the light passing away, blurred
by our stationary focus, is red.

We cannot see these colors with our eyes,
just as we cannot feel the sun pushing the stars
outward or bending the paths of their light.
Years ago when the world was flat, and then even
when the world became round, light was light,

dark was dark, and now, now that the world
is almost nothing compared with all that is—
all that we know—light identifies each atom
of the universe, and darkness swallows stars
like a whirlpool at the heart of a galaxy.

The huge magnanimous stars are many things.
We look to the sky and ask, What has changed?
Everything. But nothing we can see, and our seeing
changes nothing, until we move, and moving
we become the light of our atoms moving.

3

Spider Tumor

When you first told me about
the black silk the body spins out,
like a terrible cocoon, I imagined
her brain was like a bright field
the size of a portable movie screen
and that a white cone of light
cut through the darkness of a room
to strike the blank surface hard
with the magnified whiskers and hookworms
of dust covering the projector's lens,

and even as you explained how one side
of your mother's head would be shaved
and little X's and O's inked on her cranium
by the radiologist, and, failing that,
holes might be drilled and isotopes
lowered into her brain to lodge near
the mass, even then I thought a spider
tumor was something we might blow off
the surface of the lens or rub away
with our shirttails. But this morning,

early to visit you at your mother's house,
I reached the door as she opened it, bending
for the newspaper. Startled, she clutched
her robe and held the folded paper
to cover her wigless, rune-etched skull.
The sun caught her full on the face
and for a moment I saw how beautiful
she had always been, girlish almost,
a countenance death seemed willing to reveal.
Perhaps it was the way the sun filled

the alcove of the porch that reminded me
of years ago when I knocked at the same door
and finding it open walked quietly
into the room where your father lay
on the blue couch. And as if we were suspended
in air, he motioned that I sit by him
and hear his little wish: a large man
who wanted one more time to wade
into the cold green water of a lake, tilt
back his head and float as light as weeds.

I sat and watched him skim his hand
across the carpet and twist the nap,
like seedpods, with his fingers,
before your mother found me and eased me
from the room, the way, this morning,
she eased me past her own death, through
the room with its blue couch, to the kitchen,
where you stood wet from a shower,
a towel wrapped around your waist
and the sunlight spinning a hazy web

in your hair. And standing there,
you were no one if not your father,
or his wish to wade out of the water,
out of its mercy and forgiveness,
and dispel the weave of death
which traps and magnifies us in the past
and hides from us the brave though startled
gestures that begin each day: the hand
that reaches down to pick the paper up,
the hand that reaches out to lead us past.

For John Murphy

The Lights

Outside my father's house
I wait for him to flip the power on
and for the string of lights
we've strung over the boxwood
and pyracantha hedge to glow
and flicker in the dark waxy green
of their leaves.

We test the dead ones that lie
like buds unbloomed or bring alive
the quiet ones that need a twist
or tap, and then arrange the strand
so all the bulbs point downward.
When I feed the length to him,
his hands stretch high above

his head to measure out
the intervals for staples along
the eaves. I plant my foot
for ballast on the ladder's lowest rung
and wait for him to drive the staples in.
Across from him and through the lattice
of a climbing rose, I see, half-

etched, half-fossilized against the brick,
the stubborn ivy feet that nothing
could dissolve, a pattern radiating
like a corner of a galaxy, random
though composed of scars, traces
of pediments that held the vines
of greater mass, arteries and veins

that fed the leaves and made the circuits
vital, electrified with green,
and then returning to the ladder,
my father's shifting weight,
the insulated staples that lie white
and tangled in the box beneath
a window of cellophane, I see

the climbing rose, the lower stalks
thick and rigid with the violence
of thorns, and then my father holding up
a staple, like a wiry tooth, before he sets
it carefully over the twisted strand,
pressing hard on its head with his thumb,
until the blood drains white beneath his skin.

The Fight

When she cracked the ice tray over the spine
of the sink and lifted a spoon too precisely
from the draining board and then stirred the drink
slowly, I heard the ice cubes warning me:
This is meant for you, meant for you.

And so she cupped the plastic glass in the curve
of her hand and keeping her arm stiff, pivoted
her body and threw the drink hard at my face.
I remember thinking before the ice and vodka
hit me, *I want to remember this.* And I have,

especially the way my arm cocked back
to throw a beer bottle at her, though I hesitated
long enough that a friend could wrap me in a bear
hug and stagger me out into the back yard
where after a long time of trying to break free

of him, I sat down on the irrigation hump
that bordered the citrus grove behind the house
and stared at the black sheet of unruffled water
stretching through the rows of orange trees
with their trunks painted white and their branches

burdened with blossoms. And what emerged from the grove,
behind flickering light and sloshing water
was a man in hip boots. He stood in front of us.
In one hand he held a valve wrench and in the other
a gas lantern that sobbed and sobbed as it burned.

Treatment

Each May, often two and three times a night,
they woke to my terrible lapsing breath,
and helped me down the hall into the opaque
light of the bathroom, where slowly, out of

his sleep, my father instructed me to sit
on the toilet, hold myself straight and breathe,
while Mother reached into the glass lung
of the shower stall and turned the HOT chrome star

that sent water beating hard against the tile.
They stayed with me until the air, atomized
with steam, choked off the light reflecting
in the mirror and blurred the doorknob with silver beads.

I was alone, though I knew that Mother
sat in darkness in the hall and waited for the breath
to enlarge in me, filling each lung as if
it were the hand and fingers of a rubber glove.

And as if my parents will always be there,
sleep-disturbed and waiting in the dark, I often
sit up in my bed at night and holding in myself
some unbreathable pressure, I listen for the quiet

shuffling of their feet outside my door, for now
I know that love is little more than a constant
waking up to something harsh and almost dying,
and that it simply calls, not merely to attend

but also to cure and heal and wait, or fail,
as I thought I failed them each time I'd lose in steam
my father's shaving robe that hung blue and empty
of its barrel chest behind the door.

Territory

Under the shade of the mulberry trees,
he leans through the DeSoto's rear window
arranging samples of carpet and tile,
molding and cove base, furniture brochures
and carpet tack with its blue nails
as gnarled as shark teeth, and then he stacks

the odd suitcases of carpet squares, front to
back, back to front, their plastic handles
clicking like steel against their binding's
brass rivets. And I hear in their sad tinny echo
a question tapping its way from out of my past:
Where are the things he brought me from his world?

Where are the cardboard models of Las Vegas's
Showboat Hotel? Where is the steam that steamed
from the spout of the gigantic coffeepot
on top of the Coffee Pot Cafe? Where is the drugstore
book about the Sioux and Buffalo, and where is the child
awake at night waiting for his father to return

out of the black road of his territory and livelihood?
The child is waiting still, and he counts the trinkets
of affection he's amassed: the manufacturers' notepads
and calendars, rulers and pencils, penknives
and key chains—all those things that say where his father's
going, where he's been. And as if thirty years is only

the time it takes to walk to the front of the car,
I watch my father open the driver's door, take out
the large piñata dog, the one we hung from the clothesline,
then blindfolding ourselves swung wildly with a stick,
until we cracked its paper ribs and spilled the guts
of candies and toys into the brown dirt of the yard.

The Diver

On television my sister emerges
three meters above the water
like something carved from light,

where she balances on the springboard,
and like a graceful sleepwalker extends
her arms as counterweights. A doll

of perfect will, she rules her fear
of heights by tracing little circles
with cupped hands and then drops her arms

to start the swift wing beats of a creature
who has taught herself not to fly but to land,
more intricate than flight for the twists

and knots and folded arms that make her appear
wounded in midair, beyond recovery, though
recovery comes quickly once she clasps

her hands, entwines her thumbs to make a sieve
through which the water passes and allows
her head to enter, then shoulders and hips.

And this is how I always see her, half in,
half out of water, her body perpendicular,
toes matched, as if there is no place for

error in the world and all her body's
perfection was meant to disappear beneath
her splash—a light she carves and shatters.

Night Swimming

Last night as if I were nothing more
than a silhouette, I entered
the black water of the shallow end
and, holding my breath, I scissored
beneath the surface toward the big
round light that shimmered, steady,
unwavering, but far away, high above
the black bars of the drain.

And when I reached the light, I touched
the bright chrome rim that held it
bolted to the wall and stared
into the lens. The water like a shield
against the radiating beams allowed
me to see the live filament burning
slowly in its vacuum, the delicate
tungsten sculpted like the sharp features

of a face. Against the light my body
cast a shadow like a bat's. Then
I rose for air and hanging like a dead man
on the edge of night, or like someone
leaving the protection of a dream,
far beneath myself, I saw the drain's
crosshatch waver and then resolve
into something hard and familiar.

When I was five, alone, half-naked,
I lay on a gurney outside an operating
room and told myself I would not cry.
The walls were yellow tile, the doors
along the hall were green and closed,
and I knew that soon I'd lie again
beneath the lamp whose green eye
shone high about the watery layers of ether,

where I could hear the voices and watch,
as if through frosted glass, the large
unfocused faces bob and blur and see
the hands pass back and forth a sponge
for sweat, some bloody packing, or specimen
for biopsy. Though who at five
could know what hands were meant to hold?
Who set like a drain below the surface

of the conscious world could understand
about the thing cut out from them?
A small removal that floats and hovers
incessantly and keeps me swimming back
attracted to the light and that eventual
face, delicate, composed, so much like
my own staring up into the bright
blue operation of the day.

Naushon Island

The deer came out of the lane last night,
two bucks first and two does next—
the four at intervals. And each stopped
where the one before stopped and turned
and looked as the others looked
and then went on into the swale.

From the porch I called the dogs off
the granite rocks in the yard
where they barked at the cautious deer.
But the dogs would not come back, so I crossed
the lawn and stood with them among the rocks,
and just my hand calmed them enough

so we could watch as the deer disappeared
through the rush and grass of the swale.
I stared into the swale until the stars
above turned white, and though
I could no longer see the deer, I knew
they must lie with their legs folded,

the weight of their bodies crushing
the grass, and it was enough to calm
that portion of myself that had stopped
and turned away from the rocks
but was afraid to come in and lie down
beneath the heavy, folding rest of sleep.

Encanto Park, 1961

The Civil Defense siren wails
and sends pigeons circling the ersatz
stern-wheeler, the *Confederate Belle.*

The captain casts the bow line off and jumps
into his canvas pilothouse while the great
cool shadow of the hull swings into the channel

and sends bluegill fluttering beneath
the dock. The Evinrude sputters, purrs.
The electric motor burns its oil and turns

the phony paddle wheel that never touches water.
Somebody's birthday, though I don't remember whose
as we sit in our paper hats under the fringed

pink awning and stare ahead into a future
of landmarks and guideposts that will never change:
the white-spattered rocks and cracked bamboo

of Duck Island, the blue thumb of the band shell
that hid behind the jointed fingers of the towering
palms, and the little predictable train

that skirted the circumference of the park—
its silver engine's chuff and hoot, its dark thunder
inside the Quonset-hut tunnel. And out in the large

bowl of the cement-banked lagoon, the rented canoes
and pedal boats flash blue, red and yellow,
and shoot off white sparks of water from oars and paddles.

But all of this we saw through the glare-struck
distance of the afternoon as the *Confederate Belle*,
slow and boxy, hugged the grassy shore and near

the fragile Chinese bridge made its wide turn
that steered the prow back into its wake, which now
had almost disappeared, though something of its smooth

calm V remained so that the pilot singing loudly
from his little house could find the watery seam
and close his eyes, safe and blind for the journey home.

The Cave

I think of Plato and the limited technology
of his cave, the primitive projection
incapable of fast forward or reverse,
stop action or slo mo and the instant replay
that would have allowed him to verify,
once and for all, *Justice* or the *Good*,

such as the way my family did, hour upon hour,
in the dark, watching films of my sister
diving, going over her failures and successes
like a school of philosophers, arguing
fiercely, pulling her up from the depths
of the blue water, feet first, her splash

blooming around her hips, then dying out
into a calm flat sheet as her fingertips appeared.
Sometimes we kept her suspended in her mimesis
of gainer and twist until the projector's lamp
burned blue with smoke and the smell of acetate
filled the room. Always from the shabby armchairs

of our dialectic we corrected the imperfect
attitude of her toes, the tuck of her chin,
took her back to the awkward approach or weak
hurdle and everywhere restored the half-promise
of her form, so that each abstract gesture
performed in an instant of falling revealed

that fond liaison of time and movement,
the moment held in the air, the illusion
of something whole, something true.
And though what we saw on the screen would never
change, never submit to our arguments, we believed
we might see it more clearly and understand

that what we judged was a result of poor light
or the apparent size of things or the change
an element evokes, such as when we allowed her
to reenter the water and all at once her body
skewed with refraction, an effect we could not save
her from, though we hauled her up again and again.

About the author

Michael Collier has won several awards and fellowships for his poetry, a "Discovery" / *The Nation* award (1981), the 1988 Alice Fay Di Castagnola Award from the Poetry Society of America, a Thomas J. Watson fellowship, a fellowship at the Fine Arts Work Center in Provincetown, and an NEA creative writing fellowship.

A graduate of Connecticut College (B.A. 1976) and the University of Arizona (M.F.A. 1979), Collier has traveled widely—from London to northern Africa to Siberia and Japan—and worked at various times as a house painter and a community activist. He is an assistant professor of English and associate director of creative writing at the University of Maryland and a visiting assistant professor in the Writing Seminars at Johns Hopkins University. He was director of the summer writers' conference at Johns Hopkins in 1987 and coordinator of poetry programs at the Folger Shakespeare Library in 1983–84. His first book, *The Clasp and Other Poems,* was published by Wesleyan in 1986.

About the book

The Folded Heart was composed on the Compugraphic MCS 100 electronic digital typesetting system in Trump Mediaeval, a contemporary typeface based on classical prototypes. Trump Mediaeval was designed by the German graphic artist and type designer Georg Trump (1895–1986). It was initially issued in 1954, by C.E. Weber Typefoundry of Stuttgart, in the form of foundry type and linecasting matrices. This book was composed by Lithocraft Company of Grundy Center, Iowa. It was designed and produced by Kachergis Book Design of Pittsboro, North Carolina.

WESLEYAN UNIVERSITY PRESS, 1989